THE SACRAMENTS AS ENCASEMENT:

Jesus Is With Us

Michael J. Taylor, S.J.

THE LITURGICAL PRESS
Collegeville, Minnesota 56321

Cover design by Janice St. Marie

Nihil obstat: Michael B. Raschko, Ph.D., *Censor deputatus.*
Imprimatur: ✠ Raymond G. Hunthausen, D.D., Archbishop of Seattle, September 18, 1985.

Printed in the United States of America.

1   2   3   4   5   6   7   8   9

Library of Congress Cataloging-in-Publication Data

Taylor, Michael J.
    The sacraments as encasement.
    1. Sacraments—Catholic Church.   2. Catholic Church—
Doctrines.   I. Title.
BX2200.T29   1986   234'.16   86-18556
ISBN 0-8146-1469-8

Contents

Introduction

Like Rip Van Winkle, sacramental theologians are emerging from a very long sleep. While Christians suffered through much confusion about the meaning of the sacraments—whether they had any further value for believers in a sophisticated secular age—theologians were mostly silent or off busy with other things. Now they are back and at it again. Some new thoughts and theories are in the works. All to the good.

They say, for example, that a new sacramental synthesis is called for, one that will be less introverted and parochial, one that will pay more attention to modern thinkers—sociologists, philosophers, psychologists, anthropologists, etc. These scholars, we are told, give a truer, more up-to-date understanding of the human person, and we should develop a sacramental theology more in tune with the nature and needs of the person they describe. They say we must abandon the old "supernaturalist" mind-set and view sacraments in more human and natural terms (the two-tiered world of former days is gone forever). While sacraments help believers express their

Christian faith, they also celebrate the "grace" that is every-where present to creation. Because of Jesus, grace is "natu-ral" to the human condition. Sacraments can be healing and grace-filled encounters for believers, but the world is in need of healing and grace too, and sacraments should speak to the world at large and reveal that Jesus and his grace are ever present to it. What God wants for Christians he wants for all creation. The sacraments are becoming simpler in expression, more understandable as the faith-celebrations of the total com-munity; the days of enigmatic mystery and clerical monopoly are behind us. Who can argue?

But are the theologians forgetting (or understressing) some-thing? Could they be compounding the problem more than help-ing to solve it? To me at least they seem to understate the most important and fundamental element of all. In their efforts to surround the sacraments with socio-cultural-humanistic-scientific relevance and value, they pay little heed to the ob-vious relevancy and power they possess, and thus the sacramen-tal renewal they seek could be doomed to failure no matter what they propose. In a sense, to be of value and workable, sacraments must evoke obvious meaning and power to those who celebrate them. They must tell human beings something important, significant, and striking about their lives here and now, even before the new theories are brought in.

To me the fundamental question should be . . . is the risen Jesus with his Church or not? Is he lord and cause of its saving activity or isn't he? If it is agreed that this Jesus is with Chris-tians in transcendental mode, living with them as the lord and head of the believing community, then the next questions should be, How does he specifically show in human ways that he is here? What are his reasons for being here? How does he want us to react to his being here?

Many earlier explanations of sacraments attempted to say emphatically *yes* the risen Jesus is here! He is seen and ex-perienced as present in the sacraments. This is characteristic of "sacramentalist" Christians—they are not consumed with the idea of hearing Jesus from afar or waiting for him to come. They believe most firmly that he is here. The trouble was, older interpretations did not always explain Jesus' presence very clearly, or in ways that made sense to succeeding generations. In fact, the way belief in the realism of Jesus' presence was stated often helped to make sacraments enigmatic, even magical or superstitious actions. This is unfortunate.

Ultimately in my view former explanations failed to hold people's attention and appreciation because they did not understandably explain the most obvious first meaning and purpose of the sacraments. In emphatic ways sacraments should say that Jesus is here, not here in strange or esoteric ways testing the faith of believers, but in ways that humanly reveal his presence, while highlighting the *why* of his presence.

I have often thought it strange that many Catholics find the Mass irrelevant. "It does nothing for me," they say. Could it be that they are unaware of a simple obvious first meaning of the Mass? It is true that few explainers state this first meaning clearly, as though keeping the Mass mysterious or esoterically Jewish safeguarded its value and attractiveness. Many, looking for some mysterious or magical effect and finding none, give up on it. Actually the Mass in the first instance says and celebrates that *Jesus is here.* It's *his supper.* He invites us to come to it. He loves us in a unique way (indeed with Paschal love) and wants to tell us so and express and share his love by talking to us and symbolically touching us with his love; he wants us as his disciple-family to respond in a loving way to his Paschal love. How can we stay in love with him and he with us if we don't talk to each other and touch each other in love? Is Jesus good only as a saving abstraction? Don't we want a real live, talkative, touchable Jesus?

This short work, then, recalls an essential premise of sacramental theology: Jesus *is* with us. Hopefully, any new thinking on the sacraments will be based on this old but still valid truth.

Surely the sacraments should be more than group therapy

for the confused or cultural "rites of passage" for the pious. They should not in any way seem strange or magical. Our Jesus is not an enigmatic lord who gives us puzzles to solve. He is trying to tell us he is here and to show us why he is here. In my judgment we do little service to the cause of sacramental reform if we do not start by shouting that premise from the rooftops and making it the foundation of everything we say about sacraments.

In short, our intention is not to put down the new thinking, but to remind rethinkers not to forget the most important truth of all. Sacraments must say loud and clear Jesus is with us in all the ordinariness and complexity of life. He is here to bring meaning to our lives, all important aspects of our lives, to live and work with us, to lead us as human beings to a life fully within God's love. Sacraments are an important part of the Jesus-with-us, Jesus-for-us mystery!

1

Sacraments as "Encasement"

Most Christians believe that Jesus saves them by the authentic human life he lived and especially by his death and resurrection. In his life and in that final event Christians find forgiveness for their sins and new life in the Spirit. Sacramental theology surely begins here. Christians accept Jesus as the new Adam. He lived the truest and fullest human life. By his resurrection he has become the source of this "new life" for others. As risen and exalted he seeks to live transcendentally within believers as a vine within branches. He wants a real on-going love-relationship to exist between him and believing brothers and sisters. The indwelling is for real!

Jesus, as Son of Man, in death and resurrection entered into a transcendental mode that made a love-dwelling in him through faith possible. For Christians this is not just *theory;* it is an essential premise: "He who believes in me . . . *is in pos-*

session of eternal life" (John 5:24)—"He who eats my flesh and drinks my blood *has* eternal life" (John 6:54). In death as Son of Man, Jesus went fully into the Father's love. The Father's love went fully into the human Jesus and "that love" became transcendentally available and communicable to all who accept the exalted Jesus in faith. He seeks to bring the "love" realized in his Paschal Mystery to the world forever.

This is what "indwelling" means. Jesus and his forgiving love are with Christians. His love is within them, in their hearts. It is there to draw them more deeply into his love. This is what human life is for. It is meant to embrace and be embraced by Jesus' Paschal love. His love is there to be cherished and cultivated, but also to be "passed on." Jesus has made his indwelling in the faith community the locus of his on-going offer of love to the world. He is *within* to love. He is *within* to invite people into his Kingdom. It is a Kingdom of Paschal love meant for all.

If this is true, how does Jesus specifically show and convince believers that he is with them in love *now?* How can they know they can bring his love to others, that he wants them to do this? The word I find helpful to express how Jesus does this is "encasement." He offers his love to believers, he calls them to share his love with others, by "encasing" his love and call in symbols. Living transcendentally with believers he "encases" his presence, love, forgiveness and power in visible, meaningful symbols. In these symbols he communicates his presence and empowering love.

But this says quite a lot and it might seem an overly mysterious way of doing things. No, this is a natural way of communicating presence and love. This is how human beings do it. They are present to each other and communicate love through symbols—the symbols of their bodies and the words and actions of their bodies. They give and receive love, they transfer forgiveness and power to others by "encasing" them in symbols. To get love or forgiveness to others, to empower others, they must "encase" these transcendental mysteries in symbols which then are "sent on" to those they love, forgive or empower.

For example, if I love someone, I can encase it in words or gestures, in a gift, or in an act of service. I can verbally say, "I love you," or I can give the one I love a kiss, a squeeze or a hug, or I can say, "Accept me in my gift or service." In other words I encase my love and "send it along" *in* a symbol. If I empower a person, I send my power in a spoken or written symbol-statement. That person receives my love and power from within my "sent along" symbol. Human body-spirit persons cannot naturally get love to another body-spirit person directly; they must *encase* it in a symbol. Love—a spiritual and transcendental mystery—must be put into something that is receivable by the other, the loved one. The other then can through inner psychological mechanisms in a sense unwrap, take out of its case that *encased* love and *know* the love of the one who sent it in the symbol. Love must always be *symbolized, encased* (put in a symbol) before it can get from one human person to another. I can give it, but for it to get there and be seen and known to be there, it must be put in a symbol and be received consciously in the symbol.

Do we ever stop to think what Jesus was really doing when he spoke to people and worked his marvelous cures? The words and cures were symbolic encasements of something far more profound than informing people or relieving them of physical affliction and pain. As he spoke and drove out the "demons of disease" he was saying and showing that he could drive out the demons of sin. As he gave new life to crippled legs and sight to blind eyes, he was giving his and God's love. As the affliction was going out, sin was going out and love was coming in. Through his words and exorcisms, through his healing acts, Jesus was encasing in symbols his forgiveness and love.

Thus the exalted human Jesus, the incarnate divine Jesus living with believers in transcendental mode, seeks always to forgive and love them. As God, or as glorified man, he could give his love through some more direct mode perhaps, but he

knows how human beings know and experience forgiveness
and love. He knows how love is communicated in the human
scheme of things.

And so he chooses to encase his love and forgiveness in
symbols too and in a sense to "send them along" in these symbols. Are we just to assume or take for granted that he loves
us? Are we to have no human assurance or perception, no experience of his love received? No, we must know! We must
hear and see—in other words sensually be aware that he loves
and forgives us. In a way we must *feel* his presence and power
so that we can truly know he lives with us and that in us he
continues the work of getting his love and forgiveness to the
world.

Many Christians regard the Scriptures and the sacraments
as Jesus' major encasements of his presence and love, his call
to ministry.[1] What would believers do without the Scriptures,
where Jesus' life, words, his will are so memorably encased?
In them they can *hear* and *find Jesus*. Christians *need* the scrip-
tural encasement of Jesus' lived life and given love to know
that he is with them. But just as necessarily they *need* the sacraments. They *need*, for example, the Eucharist to know that the
Jesus who gave his Body and Blood for them is with them encasing this love in bread and wine and offering it to them. And,
as another example, the shepherd-bishop and his flock *need*
the sacrament of special ministry. How else are he and they
to know that he has been truly called to tend a flock and share
Jesus' pastor-teacher-celebrant ministry unless Jesus encases
his call and power in the approving presence of the community and in the words and hands of an already called shepherd-
minister?

Indeed, how would the human Jesus have known the
Father's love and will unless his Father had encased his love
and call in words, in felt responses to prayer, in dreams and

---

1. Chapter 6 of John's Gospel seems to give a biblical explanation of these "two
encasements" under the rubric "bread." See the Appendix to this book, p. 59.

visions, in works of power, in perceivable revelations of one sort or another? As Jesus read and meditated on the Scriptures, as he succeeded in his preaching and was enabled to work cures and exorcisms, he experienced the Father's presence. He knew the Father's love and call. This was how God encased his love and power and "sent it along" to Jesus who then psychologically unwrapped it within his soul and discovered that God was truly his Abba-Father, the one who loved him beyond measure, the one who called him to and empowered him for the messianic task.

Jesus, then, in the sacraments seeks to focus the reality of his presence and love, the purpose of his being with believers, by encasing his presence and purpose in meaningful symbols. These symbols humanly speak and confer his present love and his on-going call that the disciples join him in ministry. They show that *Jesus is here* (not "up there" somewhere speaking to or calling them from afar). He is *dwelling in* his brothers and sisters in love and power. The symbols help them know, reach and touch him *as here.* How could Christians ever realize or live the mystery of the indwelling if its encasement were not a normal part of everyday life and experience? If Jesus does not symbolically encase the mystery and celebrate it with believers, how would they ever know there is such a mystery?

Moreover, Jesus in giving love always seeks a response of love. While calling believers to ministry, he seeks their decision to undertake it. He seeks the response: "Yes, Jesus, I love you." "Yes, lord, I will minister." As his people receive, as they join in the celebration of his "sent along" love and power, Jesus receives the love of his people, their commitment to serve. As they need his love perceivably encased in symbols, so Jesus chooses to need their responding love encased in symbols too. The Jesus Story in its truest sense is a love story, the love of Jesus for the world and the responding love of the world for Jesus. Jesus "speaks" to believers and "touches" them. They must also "speak" to him and "touch" him with their faith, love, and commitment. The sacraments make this possible. They are his speech and touch and theirs too. Two-way encasement happens in all sacramental celebrations. Jesus wants it this way. But one can continue to object; the idea of encasement sounds a bit far out. How can personal love and power be encased in symbols, in symbolic actions? Isn't this making actions more powerful than they can or should be? Doesn't such an understanding of sacraments encourage superstition or magic? Can someone or something be truly, really (yes, infallibly) encased there?

Again, we must reflect on our experience and on Jesus' life as depicted in the Scriptures. In our dealings with each other we often encase our love and our "commissions to work" in symbols, in words and symbolic gestures. Our love—a transcendental mystery within—can never be known by another unless we somehow "give it" to that other. And we "give" it by putting it in symbols, in words or actions. We "send it along" in these symbols. If this is not done, the loved one, the commissioned one, never gets our love or power.

If Jesus is *here* (and shouldn't Christians believe that?), if he wishes to communicate his love and power to human persons, then he must do this in a human way. He must wrap it up, encase it in a symbol and "send it along" to those he loves and commissions. The beauty of Jesus' sent symbols is that they infallibly contain his presence. He is always an authentic and sincere symbolizer. His love and power are surely encased in his sent symbols. We, on the contrary, in our "symbol doing and sending" can be inauthentic and insincere. We can use the symbols of love but not be truly, psychologically encased in them.[2] Jesus cannot do this. He can never *not* be encased in his symbols. He means his words and actions to be the authentic encasement of his love and power and so they are. That we

---

2. It goes without saying that the so-called sexual revolution often violates the mystery of encasement by separating psychic surrendering love from the symbols naturally meant to *encase* it. What today is called "love" is often not that at all but use of love-symbols for quite selfish purposes.

are sometimes insincere in our symbol-sending cannot destroy the authenticity of Jesus in his symbol-sending.

As an example, let us say that we were physically standing before Jesus in the year A.D. 30 and that he put his arm around us in a gesture of love and said, "I love you." Would his love not be encased in his gesture and words? Obviously it would be. Why does he touch us, why does he speak to us? Precisely so that he can encase in a human way his love. We cannot get it if he doesn't encase it. Once Jesus does this, then we know because of his touch and word that he does in truth love us; the touching, the hearing have *within them* Jesus' love. And today is Jesus' love any less with believers when he (transcendentally present) offers them, e.g., the Eucharist and the other sacraments as symbolic encasements of his love?

Jesus' love is the important thing. But how can believers receive it, how can they know they have it unless Jesus "sends it along" through "word" or "touch" of some sort, or both? The sacraments are saying this. They are not inviting Christians to indulge in magic or superstition. They are Jesus living transcendentally in his Church trying to "get through" to believers in a human way with his love and call to ministry. They are Jesus "sending these mysteries along" in his chosen symbols.

It is true that Christians can be too preoccupied with the symbols and not enough concerned about Jesus being transcendentally with them "sending along" his love. The symbols are not to be isolated or given more importance than Jesus, as though they were some "love apart" and distinct from him. Still Jesus and believers know that transcendental presence alone is not enough. Because they are human, Jesus' presence must at least occasionally be *encased.* This way they become aware of it; they experience in a truly human way his love and become involved in the ministry he seeks from them.

The Eucharist is a mystery of love, not the reception of mysterious magical bread. But how is Jesus' love seen, celebrated, and received? He, Jesus, must tell believers he loves them and does so by talking to them, reminding them that he died for love of them: "This is my body given *for you*" . . . "my blood poured out *for you*." Those spoken words encase his love. But Jesus knows he must "touch" believers with his "given love" too. And so he invites them to eat the "touchable" bread and wine of his supper, encasing in that touchable symbol the supreme love of his "dying for them." It is Jesus transcendentally present who speaks the words of encasement; it is Jesus who offers believers the supper of encasement to eat. Could anyone say that nothing is there, nothing happens, that this is all empty symbol, superstitious talk? Jesus is there and his *words* encase his love. Jesus is there and the *bread and wine* encase his given love. This is what sacraments in my view say first of all. More than all else we need Jesus' love, but just as importantly we need Jesus to *tell* us he loves us. As human beings we need him to *touch* us with his love. Love left unencased is very fuzzy, abstract love. Love symbolically encased and "sent along" to us is love most real, love "most human."

2

The Sacraments: Some Reflections on Their Dynamics

Catholic tradition has long seen the sacraments as working *ex opere operato*—something really happens as the action takes place. Instinctively Catholics knew sacraments had to work this way, because they were the acts of Jesus. How could he and his love not be encased in *his actions?* He does them precisely to make his love and "call to ministry" perceivable. To say sometimes his words and gestures have loving content and power, sometimes not, is to tell Jesus he is not the determiner of the loving or ministerial content of his words and actions— we are, or something else is. On the contrary, lovers determine the value and content of their actions.

Still, while insisting on the power and value of these actions, Catholics also insisted proper believer and community involvement was important too because Jesus always respects the response mechanisms of his disciples. Sacraments were said to work *ex opere operantis*—the activity and response of the believing community are vitally important also. Jesus' encased love and bestowal of power can be refused. They can be resisted or hypocritically received without real honest acceptance. Just as Jesus' love was truly encased in the morsel of bread he offered Judas, so the betrayer's lack of love and openness rendered that love unreceivable. But could it ever be said that Judas *determined* the love Jesus put in that symbolic gesture? Certainly Jesus did not stop working signs just because people failed to see love in them. The Jesus-part of his action is always genuinely encased love, for Jesus is the encaser. The way believers receive his encased love determines whether his love "comes through" or not. The love of Jesus in itself and in his offered actions is always transforming love, but little transformation can take place if those who receive the symbols do not believe or love.

This is sound theology because it is based on common human experience. Love can be encased in symbols and is always there as long as the lover psychologically intends to put it there. True lovers seek to express and communicate love and do so by "wrapping it up," encasing it in symbols, and "sending it along" to those they love. But for this love "to get through," the loved one must always be open and responsive.

During the Reformation, Catholics rejected the position of some Protestant reformers who regarded Jesus' Eucharistic presence as happening only when the believer's subjective faith was present and working. Catholics resisted this position because they viewed the sacraments as first and foremost the actions of Jesus. He was the lord and primary agent of the Eucharistic supper. It primarily encased his love. The receiver's faith and love, which are important parts of the Eucharistic liturgy too, are in response to Jesus' love encased in the Eucharistic symbols. That the Catholic view of sacraments made more sense was indicated in subsequent history. The Eucharist continued central in Catholic tradition and practice. It all but ceased to be celebrated in many Protestant churches. If the Eucharist is the *believer's* encasement more than Jesus', why make it central at all? Why not pick any congenial symbol to encase the love of the believer for Jesus? But Catholics viewed the sacrament as quite special in that it was seen as the encasement of Jesus' own Paschal love. The Eucharist was not arbitrary or elective ritual or symbol. It was Jesus transcendentally present in the community encasing his love and inviting believers to share it. He was expressing his fullest love for his brothers and sisters as they expressed their love for him.

Surely love is in the sacramental symbols not to stay there, but to be "sent along" and "received." The container, the encasement, is the means of transferal, of getting love from the lover to the beloved. To use examples of common symbols of love, the squeeze and hug are meant to express and transfer love. Love is the important thing! To give hugs and squeezes with nothing in them is to trivialize these symbols. It can give all love-symbols a bad name. Human beings can do this with the symbols they send along to each other. But authentically given love-symbols are always containments, encasements of love. They should be seen and reverenced as such. Human beings *need* "given love" to be encased to know it is there and "coming."

Recall Catholic insistence over the centuries on the realism of Jesus' presence at Mass in the host (albeit grossly expressed at times). When celebrated in faith the sacraments of baptism, confirmation, marriage, and orders were seen as permanent, or as lasting forever. All this makes sense only if Jesus is understood to be truly with Christians, desirous to encase his love in the key symbols of the Christian community—in the waters of baptism, in the bread of the Eucharist, in the bishops who ordain, within spouses as they enter marriage. Remove Jesus from his Church, from the hearts of believers, regard the central Christian symbols of the community as not his acts but only reminders of him or stimulants to faith, then sacraments become of incidental value at best. Their value must be found elsewhere, as for example, in some socio-cultural-psychological dynamics—in their ability to incorporate individuals into groups or to promote in groups a sense of common identity, to express the group's beliefs, its "rites of passage," etc. Not denying that sacraments can have these and other complementary purposes, they must in the main be seen to be encasements of Jesus and his love if they are to hold any lasting allegiance on the part of believers. If Jesus is not perceived to be *dynamically* present in the sacraments, it is doubtful that any other desirable effects they could have will be enough to hold the respect and devotion of many Christians.

The Minister

If we accept Jesus as the present and active lord of the community, we can see why some member of the community must figure forth his presence and special saving activity.[1] His transcendent spiritual mode of presence needs to be encased in a visible believer, an appointed and approved minister of the community. This way it can be seen. It is Jesus who loves, calls, and empowers believers to carry on his saving work. But if the symbols of his love and ministry are not personally administered, his personal presence and call can go unnoticed and be unappreciated because they are not displayed.

We are not, however, suggesting a return to indulgent clericalism or stuffy ministerial order. We simply ask that Christians take Jesus' presence with the community seriously. Is he present in transcendental mode or isn't he? If he is, then the present Jesus must be seen to be in those who minister the

---

1. We speak here of the key community acts of Christian celebration, as for example, baptism, the Eucharist, anointing of the sick, etc. In their interpersonal acts of love and service, all Christians do the ministerial work of Jesus. Every Christian figures him forth to others. Still, the key community acts should project Jesus in the clearest possible terms. Jesus must be seen to be present to his Church *administering* the sacraments *personally* in the person of the minister.

key symbolic acts of his community. It must always be Jesus we see and hear, Jesus showing his love and giving his power to minister. But in our human situation, to see and hear, we need a talking, acting "personal symbol" who will render Jesus seeable and hearable in a personal way. The incarnation happened! The divine Jesus took on flesh so that he could be seen and heard, so that his divine love could be understood in human terms. In the post-resurrection mode of his incarnation, Jesus seeks still to be seeable and hearable in and through the brothers and sisters who believe in him and love him and are indwelt by him. And since Jesus is present not to overwhelm believers, but to love and serve them and, through them, to love and serve the world, the minister who figures him forth for the community should always project the image of a servant, not that of some elitist power-figure.[2]

Structure

In the Catholic tradition there has always been some fussiness over the matter of structure, maybe too much. But was there a reason? Is it important to be precise about such things? Catholics wanted to show that the present Jesus comes in very definite and particular ways. The timing and mode of his coming are important. What Jesus wants for his people in terms of love and ministry must be pinned down, spelled out, and described clearly and understandably. Symbols that unsurely encase Jesus' love and power hardly invite a dedicated response. As Paul says, "The trumpeter must sound a sure call" (1 Cor 14:8) if people are to answer it with true commitment.

---

2. Perhaps more progress could be made resolving the problem Catholics and Protestants have over the question of the valid ministry of sacraments if more stress were put on the minister as the approved "Christ-figure" who renders the present Jesus visible and hearable and less stress put on the lineal and historical handing on of ministerial power. If Christians could *agree* that Jesus is truly with the community of faith, then that community can choose members to render his presence visible for the community.

During baptism, for example, Jesus must be seen to be ministering to us. Whatever sins we have or whatever sinfulness surrounds us in the world as we approach this symbol, Jesus must be seen to be there undoing it and pledging us his strength against sin and human weakness. He must be seen to be giving us his Spirit and that Spirit to be spiritually incorporating us into his new life, the more selfless humanity of Jesus that leads to God. The baptismal action should show that we are being caught up into his death and resurrection—not fully just yet, but the mystery is beginning to happen. Baptism must indicate that we are joining the community where Jesus lives and works for the salvation of Christians and the world. This feeling cannot be "sort of there." It must be surely and convincingly there. And so "fussiness" about structure—the right words, the proper meaningful actions, the sure sense of Jesus speaking and acting in the words and actions of the minister—all this is extremely important. It should be a clear part of the baptismal symbolism.

And so with all the sacraments. In sickness, for example, Jesus must be seen to be there helping us endure it, healing the troubles of our bodies and spirits, making sure our sufferings are not lost in bitterness. He must help render our sickness in some way a redemptive and maturing experience. Sickness and approaching death present distinct temptations against faith, hope, and love. Jesus must help us overcome these and if possible get us back on our feet. When we face death, we must know he readies us for that critical moment of faith and surrender.

The structure is not the most important thing—having Jesus present is. Still, his presence and the *why* of his presence can only be seen when they are encased in sure words and meaningful actions. Jesus should not be present in some vague, general way, but in very particular ways, especially in the important and critical moments of life. The sacraments must clearly indicate that he is.

Certainly the historical Jesus was "fussy" about the struc-

ture and symbolism of his actions. He was not a vague symbolizer or a "Messiah-savior-in-general." He showed his saving
capacities in specific ways. Again, recall his miracles (and other
dramatic actions). It is John in his Gospel who calls them symbols or signs. Jesus had transcendental gifts to offer those who
accepted him as sent by the Father and who listened openly
to his words. He had heavenly gifts of life, light, and love to
offer the world. But how did he show his human audience that
this was true, since his gifts were transcendental and invisible?
He encased them in visible symbols or signs. These signs
showed forth his spiritual gifts in a human way. The inner
spiritual life he wanted to share was encased in the actions of
giving "physical life and light" to believers such as Lazarus and
the blind man and in the washing he offered the disciples (John
chs. 9, 11, and 13). The physical actions of Jesus symbolically
displayed and encased his inner spiritual love and life. His transcendental gifts were "sent along" to believers in the perceivable life, light, and washing they received. Jesus, then,
obviously encased his saving gifts in symbols when he was
historically on earth. As present in the faith community in a
transcendental mode, would he now discontinue to encase his
life and love in the faith-symbols of the community he dwells in?

Protestant Christians see clearly that Jesus encases his love
and his will in the Scriptures, in the preached and written Word.
As they read or listen to the Bible in faith, they hear Jesus,
for he is encased in those sacred words. But surely Jesus also
encases his saving presence in the key symbolic actions of his
community. As Jesus encased his love and will in symbolic actions while on earth, so he continues to do so while joined transcendentally to the believing community. Are not the historical
and transcendental Jesus one and the same? Will he not act
in the same way?

Most would agree structural reform of the sacraments is very
much in order. The sacraments must speak and show their
meaning much more obviously than they do. What has been
done so far in this regard is not nearly enough. In their word-

ing and actions sacraments must clearly indicate Jesus is present, bestowing his love and life, calling his people to ministry, and empowering them to be instruments of his saving work in the world. Sacraments should not be unduly brief or mysterious in their wording or symbolism. They must state and show Jesus' presence and purposes with obvious and moving clarity.

Sacraments and Grace

Catholic theology teaches that sacraments give grace. Can the encasement model make this belief more understandable? Surely the model calls more attention to the ever-presence of Jesus with the Church. Jesus the encaser is here! In earlier belief Catholics regarded grace as almost a quantitative something, a created quasi-divine substance which was mediated through the signs; it was understood to elevate believers to supernatural status. Since such elevation was hard to detect, the sacraments often seemed ineffective. But now grace is perceived as a relationship. Grace is God-in-Jesus giving himself. God always does this, but in the sacraments he is seen to be doing this because he encases his love in symbols which are visible to believers. In the symbols Jesus can be seen manifesting his love, encasing it, sending it along. Receiving his love encased in symbols, Christians begin to appreciate the intensity, depth, closeness, and constancy of his love. Celebrating and receiving his love in meaningful symbolic actions, they come to realize how loving Jesus is, and they begin to respond to the constancy of his love with more of their own love. This is what grace is—Jesus displays, encases, and sends along his love in expressive symbols, and believers, beholding his love, become more conscious of it, more responsive to it, and begin to live and love more like Jesus does.

Grace is also Jesus calling believers to ministry. When Jesus calls, he communicates his power to minister. Grace is Jesus loving, Jesus empowering disciples to do his work. This is why he seeks them out. He wants them to share his love and to join him in ministry. This cannot happen if Jesus is never perceived as being here or approaching believers with his love and call. The sacraments, then, are grace-giving because they are Jesus showing and sharing his loving presence. *Jesus is here* and his *present love* is always "grace" for those who are open to it!

Institution

Did Jesus "institute" the sacraments? For them to be grace-bestowing, it seems this must be the case. Most Christians believe that Jesus gave baptism and the Eucharist to his Church. The New Testament clearly shows that Jesus attached great significance and importance to these actions. Did he do this for the other actions which came to be known as sacraments? Christians differ strongly on this point. Generally, Protestant Christians find only the "two" in Scripture and so do not believe the "others" come from Christ. Catholic Christians see Jesus as "instituter" of the Church. He is transcendentally head and lord of the believing community and acts in and through the key faith-actions of the community (it is after all his Body. Christ and Christians are not separate from each other; they are one "mystical mystery" [1 Cor 10:16-17]). Jesus present to and living within his people can make known how he wishes to encase his special love for them, how he wishes to call and empower them for ministry. But sadly it seems no real agreement on "institution" can be reached until first Christians come closer to each other in their understanding of Christ and the Church. The institution of the sacraments can be solved only when Christians agree on how Jesus is present to his Church.

3

The Sacraments and Human Meaning

As believers lived and celebrated their faith, they found that (in addition to his remembered words) Jesus was particularly present to them in seven ways. In the seven ways he symbolically revealed his love. There was nothing strange or mysterious about the seven. Christians became aware of them when they were obedient and faithful to the Gospel. As they lived their lives selflessly in imitation of Jesus, they discovered and experienced his presence and love.

The seven ways also showed that a "call" goes with his love. Jesus always asks those he loves to help him with the work of his Kingdom. They must not only receive love, they must carry it to others. The Kingdom is meant for all. The seven ways, then, essentially relate to how and where Jesus and believers extend the Kingdom to others.

On reflection there is nothing esoteric about the sacraments. They are not mysterious or magical ways of discovering love or bringing it to others. Jesus' love is received and shared, his work discovered and done, when believers live their lives in a truly selfless (human) way, the way he did. Through Jesus, God tells the world how to live a truly human life. Rather than let creation haphazardly discover its meaning, God has revealed it to the world in Jesus. Since creation is intended to find its meaning in him, creation must see his presence within itself. The sacraments celebrate his presence. They reveal life's deeper meaning. What do they particularly say about life?

Baptism

Baptism reveals the true meaning of human existence. Life in its deepest sense is a journey toward God, and Jesus is the surest way to God. He is there at the start of all human life. Earthly existence is not some chance happening without meaning or direction. Jesus is its ultimate meaning and direction. As the Letter to the Colossians says, he is the first-born of all creation. All things are created through him and for him (1:15-17). He lived human life authentically and realized its fullest meaning. If our life is to be successful and authentic, it must be lived as Jesus lived it; it must be lived with him. In baptism Jesus assures the world that this can happen, that it is happening.

Baptism is not magical ritual or superstition. It is the risen Jesus coming "visibly" into one's life. Baptism is the visible symbol he chooses to encase his "coming." As we begin our journey toward God, our constant companion is to be the Paschal Christ who died and rose *for us,* the Jesus who lived life authentically and who came to the Father's love fully. In our journey, sin and selfishness will be our biggest obstacles. But in baptism Jesus, through the symbolism of cleansing water, assures us he is with us to overcome sin. He comes to forgive us and to strengthen us against sin. Furthermore, baptism, which normally takes place in a community setting, shows that we are joining the family of Christ; we are making life's journey, supported by the faith and love of many brothers and sisters. No one should make the journey alone. The symbolic rite reveals that we are one with Jesus *and* his family. This is not a desirable hope. It is fact! What better company could anyone have than this?

So Jesus must be seen as present at each new birth (or at least present when people begin to realize life is a journey toward God). He must be there at the *start* of life and throughout all of life. The sacrament of baptism says this is so. It is the symbolic encasement that reveals it is so. As believers hear the baptismal words and go into the baptismal waters, they know they are—through the power of Jesus' Spirit—entering into his life, death and resurrection (Rom 6:3-11). The symbols encase the presence and coming of the Paschal Christ. He is the baptizer. In baptism believers can know they are in the life of the most successful traveler ever! Life's purpose is what Jesus understands it to be—resurrection into God. All the world can live in union with the risen Christ and reach God as he did. This is what God wants the world to know. This is what he tells it through the baptismal symbolism.

Jesus himself, as he undertook his messianic journey to God, had to know that the Father was with him. And surely Jesus' baptism at the Jordan encased the Father's presence for him. The Father showed he was with Jesus in that event—in his "spoken" words and those of the Baptist, in the waters Jesus entered and left, in the "Spirit-dove" that descended—all these symbols were doubtless seen as encasements that helped Jesus and early Christians understand that the Father was with Jesus.[1]

---

1. Many biblical scholars see the gospel accounts of Jesus' baptism as more "theological-symbolical" than "actual-literal." Still, the images of the event as described (the remarks of the Father, the Baptist, the descending "Spirit-dove," etc.) seem to indicate that early Christians saw the baptism as having a "revelatory" significance for Jesus and for them. The human Jesus quite obviously saw the Father *revealed in many events* of his earthly life. The "theological" description of the baptism, then, would seem to correspond to the "revelatory" aspects of these events.

In a sense they made visible the Father's presence for Jesus as he began his public ministry. Having experienced the Father in these symbols, could the human Jesus doubt his presence? He must have reflected on them many times, finding in them reassurance of his Father's presence. And so Jesus wants to be with all people as they start and continue life's journey. He like the Father wishes to encase his enduring presence in meaningful symbols, particularly in the baptismal words and in the baptismal entry into and exit from water. The baptizing Jesus is, of course, the lord and head of the Church, and so people know their baptism joins them to that community. Jesus and the community seek to embrace all people and support them as they start and continue their journey toward God.

Confirmation

Confirmation makes people aware that God has built into creation "gifts of discovery" so that all who search for him can find him. In the first instance the gifts make his presence known to the brothers and sisters. They assist and draw them towards his love and closer to each other. He gives them gifts of insight and knowledge to recognize his presence and love, gifts to enable them to live the gospel openly and responsibly before others, the ability to witness him to one another and the world. Life is not a "do-it-alone" enterprise. God in Jesus works with and through believers to bring all people to himself.

Jesus must grant the world prophetic insight; he must awaken in people a social consciousness. They must be made aware that they are all interconnected and created for the same journey and destiny. The gifts are meant for all, to facilitate all to recognize God and creation's purpose and to help them make the journey successfully. They draw believers closer together. They help the world discover Christ. Jesus who spoke so prophetically of the journey's purpose while on earth must continue to speak the message forever. Christians know that he is indeed doing that. They find the prophetic, "more social"

Jesus present in the socially active community and in its "social leader," the shepherd-bishop. He and they encase the prophetic, gift-giving Jesus. From the socially conscious community he continues to call the world to an awareness of his gifts and the journey's purpose. It is true, most of God's gifts of discovery and witness come to believers in baptism. But they must be made aware of them. The gifts must be intensified and rendered more active and so Jesus does this in the confirmational mystery. The sacrament makes believers aware that like Jesus they are prophets too and can use the gifts to inform the world about God and draw it to him.

The Eucharist

The Eucharistic bread is not some magical K-rations for Christians only, but the bread given by Jesus to encase his Paschal love. This love is meant for all. It is the bread God offers the world to sustain it in the journey. Jesus must tell believers and all people that he died for love of them—"This is my body given *for you* . . . . my blood poured out *for you.*" God loves all people this much! It is good to hear Jesus tell us this. But more than a revelation of love, the Eucharist is an invitation to experience this love, to unite with it, to "touch" it. He asks the world to ". . . eat his body, to drink his blood"—in other words to know that the love that sustains the world is available to it. It is encased in a touchable symbol. If there were no audible or tangible symbols that encased this love, would the world ever know how deeply God loves it and how realistically he seeks to make his love present to it? The world needs to have Jesus' love symbolically encased so that it can realize how "total" and ever-present it is. The food that sustains the world in its journey toward God is not some general feeling that God is there and that he somehow cares. No, the world is sustained by very particular bread—the love of the Paschal Christ. It is encased in the bread and wine of the Eucharist. It is there to be seen and eaten. It is meant for all. The world "dies" without it.

Reconciliation

Through this sacrament we become aware of the two critical options we all face in life. We can be selfish and unserving, or we can be caring and open to others. Jesus is very aware of these options. By his grace and example he draws us toward good choices. He regrets how easily we follow bad ones, but he always forgives us when we do. He strengthens us against selfishness and encourages us to live more for others. To be unmindful of the injury and damage we do, to be ignorant of how self-centered and closed to others we can be, compounds our selfishness. It frustrates the humanizing process. It misdirects us in our journey. Jesus cannot let this happen. He must alert us to the stupidity and destructiveness of sin. He must be present to forgive and strengthen us against it.

That he chooses to forgive sinners in the Church shows that sin is a violation of community. It is not some private rebellion against God, a thing between him and us only; it is living solely for self instead of for the community. This violates what we are meant to be and leads nowhere.

We are members of a family. We have obligations to serve and to support the brothers and sisters by our life and example, yet, when we sin, we refuse to do so. Sin is always a scandal, an infidelity to the family. Jesus lives within this family. We cannot love and serve him unless we love and serve the family. It is altogether fitting, then, that Jesus encase his forgiving and healing presence in the injured community. This way we can in a sense "tangibly" experience his forgiveness, and we can become more aware that our sins do great harm to the community. We cannot reach God except through responsible service to our brothers and sisters. We must admit our selfish failures to them and pledge our efforts to make up for our infidelities as best we can.

Orders

People are not meant to be "rugged individualists" who travel life's journey alone; we are all interconnected. Jesus seeks always to create community. He came to Israel as a caring shepherd who sought to unite the scattered sheep into a flock. We were to come to the Father not singly but as a family. This sacrament shows that Jesus is still present in the world as community-maker.

He sends graced shepherds to feed and care for his people as a flock. He encases his teaching, pastoring, celebrating presence in those he calls and sends. The unitive work of the transcendental shepherd is encased in the unitive work of his chosen visible shepherds. We are body. We are branches. We are family. Private, one-on-one faith is not what Jesus seeks. He wants us to live the faith as brothers and sisters. Jesus, then, must make sure that his family has dedicated shepherds and teachers who will responsibly see to the spiritual feeding and unity of the flock and who will oversee the community celebrations of faith. His care and teaching is family-oriented and comes not from on high or abstractly but through the shepherds he calls and appoints (John 21:15-19).

Marriage

Marriage can be the most humanizing of all relationships. It offers people a great opportunity to work against selfishness. In marriage two people go out of self in love and in service to another. They live for the "other." And since children are a part of most marriages, this offers husbands and wives further opportunities to go out of self in love for others. As two people love and take care of one another and their children, they open themselves more radically to Jesus' love. He dwells in the others they love. He waits there to love and receive love. The human Jesus is the premier example of one who reached God through selfless love and service. Surely he must be an *essential part* of the premier institution of human love and service. Believers (reflecting on Jesus' demanding words on marriage and the clarifying insights of Eph 5:21-33) came to see that indeed he was. He was seen to be present, encased in the selfless love of Christian spouses for each other and their children. God is ever present to creation, seeking to love and be loved. Where does he most often show his love? Where does he most routinely seek love from us? Christians came to see this happen for the most part in marriage and in family life.

What happens in good marriages is what God wants to happen in all of us—that we go out in love to others. God is always out there in the ones we love. It is mostly from there that he brings his love to us. But to have marriages work this selflessly, Jesus must be with the spouses, enabling and inspiring them to take on his selfless "for others" spirit. There are many Christians who do indeed believe Jesus is encased in the spouses of all committed marriages. He resides there to inspire and facilitate the selfless love of husband and wife for one another. Their authentic love for each other is also love given him, in fact it is a reflection of his own love for the Church (Eph 5:25, 32). For most people the journey toward God is best made here. Marriage is the *par excellence* institution of family. Where the concept "family" is taken seriously, Jesus is always present.

Sickness

To be human is to know suffering. But can pain and sorrow have any meaning? Are they punishment for misdeeds, bad luck, or what? Much of our suffering comes from the way we are made. Our physical and psychic natures are subject to all sorts of upsets and breakdowns. We are free physically and psychically to hurt one another. If all we had to hope for was happiness in this life, we might want freedom from all such suffering. But this life is preface to a fuller one. Our weaknesses and limitations show us that we are not self-sustaining or complete in ourselves. We need the support and care of others; we need to support the needs and weaknesses of others. As we endure our sufferings and support others in theirs, we learn how to give and receive love. Human persons find fulfillment as they go out selflessly to others. They are fulfilled as others come to them in their need and weakness.

Surely the human Jesus knew suffering. He sought God's help to bear it. He was consoled by the understanding and comfort people gave him. His weakness and limitation drew him to seek the love of others. The weakness and suffering of others drew him to go to them with whatever love and help he could bring them. Jesus was above all a person "for others." This is why he is the Savior. In assisting the needs and sufferings of others, he was able to find the fullness of God. As the human Jesus went fully out of self for others, God came fully into him and fulfilled him completely. It is this saving "fullness" that he shares with us (Phil 2:5-11; Col 1:19-20, 2:3-4; Eph 4:13; John 1:16).

Jesus knew pain and sorrow. He is not indifferent to ours. He knows he must be with us as the Father was with him. We are often weak and need healing. In our sufferings we lose our direction. He must come to redirect our steps so that we continue the journey in faith and hope and without bitterness. The sacrament shows the healing Jesus is with us in sickness and suffering. He is perceivably present in the love of our families, in the concern and care of the community, in the consoling presence and words of the minister, in the soothing anointing of oil. Christians see these as the symbols that encase Jesus' healing love for those who suffer. The sacrament shows that no part of human experience is wasted. It can be humanizing in unsuspected ways. Jesus showed us this. As we endure our sufferings supported with his presence and love, our sufferings (like his) can be redemptive. They can draw us out of prideful independence and bring us closer to him, the Father, each other.

Death

Death is not the senseless end of a life. It is the time of arrival. All of life takes on importance and meaning in light of this critical moment. We are on a journey. We live and travel so that we might arrive successfully. When the destination has been reached, Jesus who has been with us through all of life, will surely be there at the end. He is the gate we go through to reach the Father (John 10:2, 8-10; 14:6-7). Resurrection into him and the Father is our destiny. For Christians Jesus is above all the resurrection and eternal life (John 11:25-26). The world must never be allowed to forget this great truth. And so the transcendental Jesus must be seen to be perceivably present with the dying, leading them to resurrection. Christians know he is with them in this critical moment—they *see* him encased in the caring community, in the minister and the soothing symbols of the sacrament. Only Jesus can bring us to the Father (John 14:6).

Conclusion

To celebrate the sacraments is not to indulge in superstition or magic. They celebrate the presence and love of the risen Jesus. It is good to know the transcendental Jesus is with Christians spiritually. It is even better to know that his presence and love are often encased in symbols. This way they can see, hear and touch him. Presence and love that are not encased can go unnoticed and be unappreciated. Furthermore, in the sacraments Jesus calls believers to help him bring his love to the world. Sacraments are commissions and empowerments. Jesus works through believers to get to others; he gives them enabling power to bring him to others. Christian history bears out this "vocational" understanding of sacraments.

Moreover, sacraments reveal the deeper meaning of life. Again, recall the example of baptism. To be born into the world, to share human life with others, to know earthly joy and hap-

piness, to have friends who love us is good. But to be born
into a world that is destined to share not only human love but
also God's love now and forever is far better. Baptism shows
us that this is indeed life's deeper meaning—the world is called
to live with Jesus, to be born into his life, to know the Father's
love as he did. Would any of us suspect this deeper meaning
and destiny if Jesus were not perceived to be present with us
as we start life's journey?

Human life should not be a question mark. People should
not wonder about its meaning. They should know it has glorious
meaning and purpose. Life is a journey toward God. Jesus seeks
to make the journey with us, to draw us into his love. It is there
that the Father's love is fully found. But as free creatures we
know we can be selfish and closed to others. Jesus must be
with us to help us live and love in more selfless ways. In baptism we see not only that Jesus comes to us, but that he also
places us in a community that views life's journey as he does.
Here he further helps us to go out to others in love and service. When we do that, we always find God's love. It is in the
others we serve; his love comes to us from there. It is this love
that truly fulfills and completes us. Human life is a learning
process. We must spend our days working to become more
selfless. And the sacraments show that Jesus and our brothers
and sisters are with us in this effort. We are not alone. We help
and support one another in the learning-to-love process. It is
good to know this.

As we celebrate the sacraments together, we become more
and more aware of the familial nature of human existence. The
sacraments are not private rendezvous with God. They are
family celebrations. They show that we are all making the same
journey with the same Christ. We are all learning how to love
together. We are meant to help, support and serve one another
in this common effort. Jesus at least has not given up on family.
He knows this is where most human growing and learning take
place. When we learn to relate selflessly to others, that is when
we are most human.

As Jesus celebrates his presence in the sacramental signs, we realize that we are one with him who reached the Father's love fully through his death and resurrection. The risen and glorified Jesus lives with us. He has come to share his life, to make us his brothers and sisters. By this sacramental "coming" he visibly assures us that we are destined to live forever with him in the Father's love.

Of course as free persons we can go our own way. We can choose a path of self-love. It is difficult to travel Jesus' way to the Father. Can we actually stay with him and reach the Father? The sacraments show that Jesus is committed to that eventuality. In the sacraments he reveals over and over again that he stays with us no matter what. He is with us through all of life. He supports us every step of the way. And since the sacraments are also Jesus calling us to ministry—a ministry that charges us to bring him to each other and the world—we know that Jesus seeks to bring the world to the Father too. What the sacraments eloquently display to Christians, God wants for all.

4

Sacramental Spirituality

Do believers in this day and age need the sacraments? Christians through history have often used the sacraments in superstitious ways. Some have understood them to work almost magically. Perhaps the time has come to set them aside as excess baggage. Faith in Jesus, knowledge of the Scriptures, living commitment to the commandment of love—the formula has worked for many. Believe in Jesus. Read and study the Scriptures. Listen to them with an open mind and heart. Attempt to live their message. What more do Christians need than this?

No one should discourage faith rooted in the Scriptures (God speaks in and through those words; they are "encasements" too). But can there be a danger here? Can an exclusive Scripture-oriented, sacrament-free spirituality encourage an exaggerated "individualist" faith at the expense of other important elements of Jesus' message? The relationship of Christians to Christ is more than one-on-one. Christians are *members* of his *Body*. They are one of many branches of the invisible vine. They are all interconnected. To be a Christian is to be spiritually related to all Christians, a potential brother or sister to every human being on earth. Jesus is not just personal savior. Believers come to him by joining a redeemed community. They belong to a family. They should strive for a spirituality that accepts Jesus as one who seeks to live in all and who loves all—the good, bad, indifferent, bright, dull, those of one denomination, those of all denominations. Believers cannot love and serve him while excluding others from their love. What they do to others, they do to him.

Certainly, then, the sacraments are important for a believer's spiritual life. Christian spirituality is essentially interpersonal, communitarian, familial. The expression "brothers and sisters" is not a meaningless piety. It lies at the heart of the Christian message. Sacraments help believers realize this. They invite them to live and celebrate the faith together as a family. They keep Christians from "individualizing" their faith to an exaggerated degree.

Recall Paul's Letter to the Corinthians (1 Cor: chs. 1, 10, 11 especially). He considered the problems at Corinth very serious. For one thing, their conduct at the Eucharist violated their spiritual *unity*. The supper should have taught them that they were brothers and sisters of Jesus. The meal was a celebration of their spiritual oneness with him and each other. Sharing the symbol of the one loaf, they should have seen that Jesus was present forming them into one Body, a family. But their divisions and selfishness contradicted this unity. Sacraments reveal that Christians are a family. They charge them to live and act like a family. Had the Corinthians been more informed and authentic in their sacramental life, they would have been more authentic in their moral conduct (their spiritual life).

As Paul further explained the meaning of the Lord's Supper, it became apparent that many Corinthians did not appreciate the love Jesus had "encased" in that meal. He was not an absent lord loving them from afar. He was present at the supper. The Eucharist, Paul reminded them, was Jesus' Body and Blood. He had given his life for them and had encased his love in the bread and wine of the Eucharist. This was the "food" he offered them—his Body and Blood, his surrendered love, his very self. Sacraments are revelations of Jesus' love. They show that he is present, that he encases his love for believers in meaningful symbols and offers it to them. Love is a transcendental thing. For believers to know and realize it, it must be encased in symbols and "sent along" to them. Sacramental spirituality calls Christians to respond to Jesus' love. But his love is not a general, abstract, or distant love. It is a present love, an encased love, a love made "visible," "hearable," "touchable."

Moreover, receiving the food of Jesus' Paschal love at a family gathering, the Corinthians should have realized Jesus' love was not just a personal gift. His love was given to create and sustain the Christian family. If they had understood and celebrated the Eucharist properly, they would not be indulging in factionalism and selfishness. Celebrating and sharing Jesus' selfless love, they would be drawn to more selfless love of each other. An authentic and informed sacramental life always inspires an authentic spiritual life. Christians are one spiritual Body in Christ. They must act like one. As Paul teaches over and over again, Christians must live lives "worthy" of the love they have received (see, for example, 1 Thess 1:11; Phil 1:27; Eph 4:1, etc.).

The same letter gives a further example of conduct Paul deplored. He viewed the situation as very unchristian—the case of the man living openly in incest (1 Cor 5). This man lived as if his conduct had nothing to do with anybody else. Others paid small heed to what he was doing (in other words, they acted as if Christian morality were a private matter). To Paul this was all wrong. Such indifference was a violation of their spiritual unity in Christ. They acted as if sin were a personal, not a *family* problem. Paul, however, insisted the *family* do something about the sinner and his sin. *They* should seek to save this man. *They* should get him to repent and do something about his sin. In the first instance Paul urged the temporary separation of the sinner from the family (serious Jewish sinners of the time often "encased" their sorrow and repentance this way: temporary excommunication revealed the selfish and anti-community nature of sin).

In the Second Letter to the Corinthians (2:5-11), Paul urged the family to bring an excommunicated sinner back to the community. In that case Paul thought the sinner had expressed sufficient sorrow. They were now to "encase" forgiveness of the sinner in an act of loving reconciliation with the community. Acknowledgment of sin, repentance for sin, and forgiveness of sin were understood by Paul to be a family problem calling for a family solution. Of course they were not doing this on their own apart from Jesus. He was with them. All these acts were done "in his name" (1 Cor 5:4-5; 2 Cor 2:10-11). In these two cases Paul seems to suggest a sacramental response to the problem of serious sin and how it should be forgiven. Authentic sacramental celebration brings home to Christians the nature of sin, its damaging effect on the community, the need for rehabilitating sorrow on the part of the sinner, and the need for final reconciliation of the sinner with the family. Christian morality is family morality. When sin threatens it, the family should be involved. It should be caring, but also responsible, seeking to "save the erring brother." To sacramentalize sorrow and forgiveness is not a superstitious, unchristian thing to do; it seems the authentic natural Christian thing to do.

Today this might seem like pious meddling in the lives of others. But is it? Is Jesus present in the community? Are Christians really branches of the vine—members of his Body—truly one spiritual family? If not, then Paul's advice is meddling. But if, on the contrary, believers are one spiritual family, then his advice is well taken. It is a sacramental display of "who Christians are"—"what sin is and does"—"what the family should do about it." While looking out for the salvation of the "erring brother," they must look out for the good of all the brethren. To do nothing shows little love for the family or the sinner. If Jesus has made Christians his Body, then it is *in them* and *through them* that he encases his love and forgiveness. Sin is a violation of the mystery that says Christians are a mystical community in Christ. Sinners should express their sorrow for compromising or violating the mystery *here*. They should seek forgiveness for their sins *here*. Paul understood that.

When we ask if a devout and informed sacramental life can inspire an authentic Christian spirituality, we could well reflect on what is happening to marriage today. Divorce becomes ever more commonplace. Why? Many fail to see in the relationship anything uniquely religious or Christian. It is just something people do instinctively and naturally. As they advance in years and mature intellectually, sexually, and emotionally, people want to "settle down," earn a living, and have lasting relationships. They seek friendships that will satisfy and fulfill them more than passingly. All in all marriage seems a good and natural thing for independent young adults to do. They enter it hoping for the best. If it works out, fine; if not, other "relationships" can take its place.

But what if the relationship is more important than that? What if Jesus thinks marriage is ideally suited to teach life's main lesson—how to love selflessly? This is what life is really about. Human persons are born for God's love but can never come fully into it unless they learn how to love selflessly. Marriage enables them to love this way, for ideally married people are trying to love each other selflessly.

And moreover, what if Jesus informs us that marriage is where he chooses to "dwell"—that his love, when we are married, comes to us through the selfless love of a committed spouse—that our love is given to him through the selfless love we give our spouse? In other words, what if marriage is a sacrament? Jesus is here. He lives within loving husbands and wives. He encases his love in the selfless love married Christians give each other. If people saw marriage in this light, they would surely undertake it with more seriousness. Divorce would be a last resort, not the easy option always so close at hand.

Surely Jesus taught the seriousness and importance of marriage. It had a much deeper meaning than people realized. He scandalized them when he insisted marriage was put together by God and was to "last forever." Marriage is the chosen vocation of most people. It is where most will live the better part of their lives. If they are to learn how to love selflessly, this is where it will happen. Marriage asks two people to open themselves to each other, to give committed love and service to one another. The selfless love and service they receive from each other will be more fulfilling than any other human love they will know. For this to happen (since human beings can be so selfish) Jesus would *have to be* part of marriage. Selfless love of others is how people get to God. This is Jesus' specialty. He knows how to love this way. In the marriages of his disciples, he pledges his presence and help to teach them this manner of love.

To say marriage is a sacrament is to say that Jesus is there: his love is encased in the committed and selfless love of Christian husbands and wives. God's love can best get through to people when they are truly open to others, when they are selfless and serving in their love. Since marriage aspires to this kind of love, God must be its author, and Jesus, the incarnation of his love, must be an essential part of it.

The author of Ephesians speaks of marriage as a "great mystery" (5:32). In the Pauline sense of the word "mystery," this would mean marriage is an essential part of God's plan to bring the world to his love. It is that important! As "mystery" it must be a sacrament, a vocation undertaken with and for Jesus. His selfless love is its foundation. Married love can succeed only when it takes on the selfless character of Jesus' love.

Spirituality and Encasement

When Jesus was historically on earth, he often encased his presence and love in symbolic words and actions. Should Christians now tell the transcendental and glorified Jesus to discontinue this approach—it is superstitious—Christian spiritual life no longer needs his presence and love "encased" in symbols? Christian revelation tells believers when they give faith to Jesus they are born into a new life (John 3:3-9). It says they enter into a spiritual love-relationship with him and the Father. Are contemporary Christians to assume this is so on Jesus' word only? Can they have no sensible symbolic assurance that this is so? Would not Jesus now, as during his earthly mission, want to "encase" the mystery of his love (the "new birth") in a symbol so that believers could be aware of it in a humanly perceivable way? How can believers live their lives in response to his love if they cannot somehow "see" and "feel" it? Surely Jesus would want to encase this love-relationship in a meaningful symbol so that believers can know they are in truth in that relationship. Christians from the beginning have believed that Jesus "encased" this relationship in the waters of baptism.

Christian spirituality is based on the revelations of Jesus. He brought God's life-giving and liberating truth to the world. But it is good to remember he often chose to encase the truth he revealed in symbolic actions. This made his truth more understandable, more perceivable. When the spiritual truth he revealed was encased in visible symbols, it was then that disciples often came to see and believe in its true reality.

Recall the example of the blind man in John's Gospel (ch. 9). Jesus promised him eternal light—an invisible and spiritual reality. How could this simple man know that Jesus had such light to give and in fact could give it? Note how Jesus communicated his eternal light to the blind man. He did not give it to him directly (by infusion as it were). He *encased* his new life and light in the "human vision" he gave the blind man. Jesus spoke words—he performed visible actions—he imposed

hands—he made an ointment and anointed the man's eyes—
he sent him into the waters of Siloam—the man came out "seeing." Jesus gave the man his "spiritual light" (the new birth),
encased in the symbols of his words and actions.

A further example of encasement is in the foot-washing epi-
sode in the same Gospel (ch. 13). Jesus was insistent about this
washing. He said the disciples must let him wash their feet;
otherwise they could have no part in his love. Jesus' love is
a transcendental spiritual mystery. It is a psychic reality within
Jesus. But how can the disciples know they have it? First, Jesus
encases his love in the historical event of the Paschal Mystery—
his suffering, dying, and rising. His psychic love is encased in
that event. It is now "seeable," "beholdable." What Christian
could look at that event and fail to find love there?

But is that great encasement enough? When it happens are
the disciples to assume they are part of it? Jesus apparently
thought more was needed. The love he encased in that historical event must be further encased and "brought to" the disciples. They must be *touched* by this mystery themselves. And
so the foot-washing (it seems a clear reference to Christian baptism) is Jesus' encasement of his Paschal Mystery. Jesus not
only loves the disciples; the Paschal Mystery shows that. But
he also encases his Paschal love in the symbol of foot-washing
and washes them with that symbol.

Love is the key mystery Jesus wishes for the disciples, but
he knows something additional is necessary. For the disciples
to know and feel his love, it must be encased in symbols like
a washing, a touch, a word, an anointing, a life-giving cure,
etc. It is in the "hearing" and "touching" that love comes
through and is realized. Christians should read the Scriptures
for spiritual direction, by all means. But they should notice as
they read the Scriptures how often Jesus encased his love and
forgiveness in sensible symbols. It was in the symbols that believers discovered his inner spiritual gift of love. Spiritual life
is predicated on Jesus' love; it is the life the disciples live in
response to his love. Sacramental spirituality finds this love en-

cased in symbols. Love not encased can go unnoticed and be unappreciated. Unencased love is difficult to respond to. Jesus knew this then. He knows it now.

When Jesus had ascended and was no longer perceivable in a personal way, the New Testament refers frequently to the "gifts" believers received "in his name"—for example, the gifts of healing, the ability to preach the Gospel with great conviction, the gifts of prophecy, insight, tongues, interpretation, etc. These "gifts" seem to be further examples of encasement. Jesus was showing believers he was still with them. The gifts encased his presence and power. Christians continued his work on earth not alone but with him. The gifts were further proof of that.

Sacraments, the symbols and symbolic activity in which Jesus encases his presence and love, help Christians develop an authentic spiritual life. It must be remembered that Christians are not just spiritual beings. They are made of flesh and blood. They not only need to know in an intellectual way that Jesus loves them, they also must "feel" his love, experience in a symbolic but human way his presence and power. People know spiritual reality in and through symbolic communication. Christian spirituality is based on the belief that Jesus is present with believers. They try to live in a selfless way not only because he asks them to but because he is with them helping them to. The sacraments celebrate this presence symbolically.

The sacraments in a sense open up and continue the great incarnational event. God took on flesh so that people could see and hear and experience his forgiveness and love in a way natural to them. He continues to make himself seeable, audible, and touchable in the sacraments. They celebrate his incarnation over and over again. They show Christians that the incarnation has been opened up to include them. Disciples not only *behold* the sacraments—they *receive* them. As he encased his life in the human flesh he assumed, so he continues to encase his presence and love in these seeable, audible, and touchable symbols. The world first sensually experienced the "spirituality" of God in the "corporality" of Christ's flesh. Christians continue to experience Jesus' "spirituality" in the "corporality" of the sacramental symbols. They encase his spiritual presence and love.

Encasement: A Further Value

It is good to know that Jesus encases his presence and power in symbols. People are thus able to know and sense his presence in a human way. Would the sacraments understood as encasements prove helpful in another way? Surely they help Jesus get through to believers on a level more natural to them. Would they serve a further purpose? It would seem so. The symbols enable Jesus to encase and protect his essential meaning for believers. Christians have a tendency to make him what they would like him to be. But Jesus is Jesus. His work and presence have an absolute and eternal meaning and value. The purpose of his life and work should not be a question mark or an enigmatic puzzle that only theologians can decipher. He is and was God's Son. He is the Savior of the world. He must not let people distort his identity or the meaning of his mission and message. What he did and is doing for the world should not be lost in the density of theological speculation or the pieties of subjectivism. Nor should the relativists and individualists be allowed to pervert his meaning at will. Jesus is Jesus. He must continue to be the world's Savior. He must continue his saving works. He must show the world he seeks to draw it into his Father's love. The sacraments help him do this with clarity and sureness. In the sacramental symbols Jesus continues to teach believers who he is, what he has done for them and the world, what he seeks to do for them, what he wants of them. They show Jesus lives with believers; he is present helping them live their lives more selflessly. His efforts are ever directed at forming them into a family. When they live like a caring and loving family, he can bring them safely home to his Father. If Jesus then speaks surely about himself, believers, life's purpose, in the sacraments, what particularly does he say?

Baptism

Here Jesus tells believers he offers them a new birth in the Spirit. Through the power of his dying and rising he can bring them into his Paschal love. In this love they find the forgiveness of their sins and strength against evil. They become members of the family of God. They possess God's life and are destined to know his love forever. In their lives they are to be more selfless and caring because they live within the selfless and caring Christ. They are to live, pray, and act always as people joined to Christ. In baptism Jesus tells believers the "indwelling" is for real. They must live accordingly.

Confirmation

Here Jesus reminds believers of the great responsibilities of their baptism. What he gives them is meant for all people. In the sacrament he more solemnly "sends" them to tell the world about his Paschal love. They have gifts that enable them to be "prophets" of this love to others. Confirmation makes believers aware that Christian spirituality always involves the good of others.

Eucharist

Here Jesus calls believers to the meal of bread and wine that encases his Paschal love ("come . . . this is my body and blood given for you"). As they share the meal in faith they become more conscious of their spiritual oneness with Jesus and each other. The disciples of Jesus are a Eucharistic family; they share in Jesus' Passover and must bring his Paschal love to each other and the world. True Christian spirituality is realized when believers try to live what they celebrate here.

Reconciliation

Here Jesus informs believers that sin is not just private selfishness or rebellion. Christians are a family. The sins of one affect all. They make the common journey toward the Father all the more difficult. Christians are supposed to support each other by the good example of their lives. The sinner refuses to do this and instead cares only about self. Jesus, then, would have believers submit their sins to the family. They should express their sorrow to the community injured by their sins and seek reconciliation and forgiveness. Sin is never just a private moral lapse; it is always a "family problem." Moral acts are good or bad as they do hurt or do good to others. It is important for believers to know this.

Orders

If Jesus saves believers by forming them into a family, he must see to it that they are cared for in a provident family way. He must continue to teach and inspire them with authority. Like a good shepherd he must protect, feed, and guide them. Jesus is present with the family as "the teacher," "the pastor," and "the celebrant of faith" in the visible shepherds he calls and empowers. Through them he continues to teach and inspire a selfless faith. It is true all Christians providently look out for each other. Still, as *family,* Jesus provides the flock with special graced shepherd-leaders. The family's journey toward God should be an *ordered* one.

Marriage

Marriage, the human institution of committed love and service, surely must involve Jesus! More than anything else, an open and selfless committed love for others enables people to receive God's love. Married love aspires to be open and committed. Believers, then, enter marriage knowing that Jesus must be an essential part of their love. The sacrament says he dwells in married believers so that they may develop a more selfless and serving love. He helps them love this way. Their task is to let his love shine through to the rest of the family.

Sickness, Death

All people know suffering, sickness, and death. Can such things have any meaning or value or salutary purpose? Can suffering draw people closer to each other and to God? Jesus knew suffering. He experienced death. In his suffering he not only came closer to God; he came fully into God's love. He must show believers that they can find God in their sufferings too. Even suffering can purify and draw them closer to God. Jesus is there. He encases his presence in the caring ministry of the community. With Jesus and the consoling community present, believers can direct even suffering and death to God. The "emptying process" must take place before God's fullness can make total entry. And as the Father was with him in his suffering, so Jesus assures believers he is with all who suffer, supporting them in the purifying process.

Jesus seeks to make people more selfless. More than all else, he wants believers to be a caring and loving family. But how can they know this if Christians never symbolically celebrate that they are a family? Christians are at their best when they look and act like family. They look their worst when they treat each other as strangers or enemies, as though they were unrelated. Christians are not individuals "going it alone" with Jesus. They are Body-members of Jesus, branches of the vine. Sacraments reveal and celebrate this spiritual fact.

Most Catholics instinctively worry about other Catholics who give up on the Mass and the sacraments. Why? Because they seem to have lost all sense of family. They prefer to go it alone. They love Jesus, he loves them—that's it. They seem to have no further need of the family. It is true that Jesus loves them. But how did he conclusively show his love? In general and unspecified ways? Or did he show and climax it in a very particular act of love? Did he die for them? Rise for them? Does he invite them as he invites all the family to share in his Paschal love? The Mass is Jesus' symbolic encasement of this love. To be indifferent to it, to disregard Jesus' invitation to celebrate the symbolic encasement of it with him and the brothers and sisters would seem to say that these people have lost sight of Jesus' special love for them. John's Jesus calls the disciples "consecrated" (John 17:18-19). They were "consecrated" not by some abstract heavenly anointing, but by his "hour," that is, by the particular love he showed for them in his dying and rising. It is because they are consecrated by his Paschal love that he can now send them into the world to carry on his work. That some are indifferent to such a "consecration" and "sending" and that they would want no part in it is a sad "falling away" indeed.

Conclusion

More than all else, the sacraments say that Jesus is here! He lives with his consecrated and sent family. Christian life and service, Christian spirituality, are based on the indwelling presence of Jesus with his people. Eschatology is realized! The end of the world is *now!* Jesus has come!

Sacramentalist Christians can never be present at a baptism and say nothing happens—celebrate a Eucharist and say Christian fellowship might be here but not Jesus—witness a marriage and say it is a secular contract and nothing more. To say such things would be to deny the uniqueness of the incarnation. It would be to say the world is not affected at all by Jesus' life, death, and resurrection. It would be to say that Jesus has not returned. On the contrary, sacramentalist Christians put no such limits on the Paschal Mystery and its saving power. Not only has Jesus returned, but he constantly celebrates his return in the sacraments. They encase his here-and-now presence, love, and power.

To say this is not to limit his presence to the seven sacraments. The glorified Jesus is with Christians in limitless ways.

To know these many ways belief in his sacramental presence in the key signs and symbols is most important. These signs and symbols show he is surely with Christians in the most important and significant times of their lives. Life's journey toward God is never traveled alone. Jesus is always there. And he is there not just to get believers home to God but also to inform them he has work for them to do. Present in his special symbolic acts, Jesus also encases in these acts the mystery of his sending. In the sacraments he makes believers his consecrated people and sends them to witness him before the world. They must bring his Paschal love not only to each other but also to the world at large. He gives them power to do this.

The sacraments, then, are not excess baggage for a modern, sophisticated age. They are encasements of Jesus, his presence, love, and power. As noted, presence and love that are not encased can too frequently go unnoticed and be unappreciated. The sacraments reveal Jesus' presence in seeable, hearable, and touchable images. They tell believers who Jesus is, what he's done for the world, what he wants for the world. They charge believers to live this revelation and to bring news of it to the world. Christian spirituality surely begins here. Jesus is in the world and he encases his "hereness" in the sacraments. If Jesus is not here in a perceivable way, inspiring us and helping us to live and love more selflessly, how can we ever lead a truly human and meaningful life, how can we ever make it home?

5

A Final Word

As exalted and glorified Jesus lives with believers in a transcendental mode. Since this mode of presence is spiritual and invisible, he makes believers aware of it by encasing it in visible symbols and symbolic activity. He did not leave Christians a full complement of magical charms that produce mysterious and powerful effects. More properly, Jesus *leaves himself.* He has returned. He is here and lives with believers! He shows he is here by encasing his presence, love, and power in symbols that his disciples can see, hear, touch, and respond to. They are body-spirit people. Jesus communicates with them as they communicate with each other, through seeable, audible, touchable symbols (this is the natural language of body-spirit people).

When sacraments are understood as the symbolic actions of Jesus, believers are able to grasp with greater realism his closeness to them; they become more aware of the depth and extent of his love. He loves them not in vague and general ways; he loves them with Paschal love. He has given his life fully for them and wishes to bring his love to all aspects of their lives. The sacraments encase this love; they extend it to every aspect of life. They are Jesus' invitation to come, see, hear, touch, and have his love.

As sacraments encase Jesus' love, they can also encase the believer's faith and love. This is an important part of the sacraments. Jesus is present in the symbols offering his love. But he seeks and must have a response to his offering. The sacraments give believers a most appropriate way of responding to Jesus. As sacraments provide him a way of "giving" his love in a perceivable form, they also provide believers a beautiful way to "give" their faith and love to Jesus. In fact, for Jesus' sacramental love-initiative to work, it needs the faith-love response of believers. His love cannot get through to them unless their faith-love comes through to him. Jesus encases his love in the sacraments so that he can "send it along" to believers. They too must encase their faith and love so that they can send them along to Jesus. The sacraments are the most apt instruments for this sending.

Salvation is knowing Jesus' love. To know his love people must open themselves to him through faith. They must give their love to him. As we know, faith and love are transcendental spiritual realities. When they happen, they happen within a person's soul and spirit. But human persons are body-spirit people. When they believe and love in their hearts, they have a need to "encase" these spiritual happenings in sensible symbols so that they can send them along to Jesus. It is instinctive and natural for people to do this. Human believers and lovers cannot keep faith and love locked up in their hearts; they must somehow embody and encase them (put them in symbols), so that these inner transcendental realities can be sent on to the one they trust and love. If they do not symbolize in words and actions what goes on in their hearts, they can well wonder if anything went on there.

Believers say in their hearts, "Jesus, I accept you, I love you, I surrender my life to you." But how can they best embody and encase this inner spiritual conversion? Baptism (at least in the case of adults) seems the most appropriate first way to encase their acceptance, love, and surrender. Believers spend much time in study and prayer as they prepare for baptism. They come to understand it as the place where they are to meet Jesus. They long to embrace the symbols in which he will encase his love. They go to those symbols freely and willingly. In their hearts they have told Jesus, "I believe, I love, I want always to be a part of your life." In the symbols of baptism they encase what they have said in their hearts. Their preparation for and submission to baptism is the sending along of their faith and love. As Jesus in the symbols "sends" his love to them, so they in the same symbols "send" their faith and love to him.

Christians know and believe that Jesus gave his love fully for them in death. They also know and believe he rose and has spiritually returned to share this love with them. The Eucharist as a sacrament says that Jesus and his Paschal love are encased in the meal of bread and wine. Jesus wishes believers to share in this supper; it is for them. "Come, eat and drink. This is my body given, my blood shed. My fullest love for you is here." Do they believe this? Do they really love Jesus who suffered, died, and rose for them? Of course they do. But is it not most important that they embody this belief and love? They should joyfully and freely come to the Eucharist. They should partake of the meal with gratitude. Surely their coming and sharing in the Eucharist is the best way to encase their faith and love. Devout and honest Eucharistic participation is the most appropriate means of sending their faith and love to Jesus.

And so for all the sacraments. Believers should not come to them abstractly or passively. They should celebrate them knowing that Jesus is there encasing his love for them. They should celebrate them as active encasements of their own faith and love. The sacraments are the coming together of Jesus and believers in symbolic exchanges of love. No one should go to a baptism or to a Eucharist (or to any sacrament) as a "receiver" only. They should be "givers" too, encasing in the sacramental symbols their inner faith and love. The sacraments, in fact, assume that believers are doing this. Jesus' love cannot get through unless people believe and love. His love is always surely present. The believer's love must be present too. The sacraments provide a most beautiful way of encasing this love and making it present.

Furthermore, as was said earlier, the sacraments are the faith-love celebrations of the Christian family. Christians make life's journey to God not alone but as members of Christ's spiritual family. Individual Christians are supported by the faith and love of many brothers and sisters. In a very real sense the sacraments encase the family's presence, their faith and love also. Jesus is present actively loving. The believer, the brothers and sisters, all are present believing and loving. The sacraments perhaps better than anything else help Christians celebrate what they are—a family. They are a people who have given common faith and love to Jesus and who come together in unity to encase this faith and love in the symbols that also encase Jesus' love for them. As Paul told the Corinthians (1 Cor 10:16-17), Jesus and believers are one "mystical" Body and the sacraments (most particularly the Eucharist) celebrate this spiritual fact.

Appendix

Jesus the Bread of Life

A Commentary on Chapter 6 of John's Gospel

*John calls Jesus the Word (1:1-18). This could mean that he
sees Jesus as the incarnation of divine Wisdom who comes from
heaven to reveal God and his will to the world. As the Word
made flesh he makes God humanly perceivable. When people
come to him, they see and hear God. But is Jesus only this—a
revelation of God in human terms? No, he is much more. He
wants to share his life and love with the world. When people
listen to his words and believe them, they receive life. When they
seek his love, they find it. In a sense Jesus offers the world two
life-giving breads—the bread of his revealing Word (Jesus as Wisdom) and the bread of the Eucharist (Jesus' Paschal love encased in the symbols of the supper he leaves his disciples). If
believers eat these two breads, they find the spiritual nourish-
ment Jesus offers the world—his life and love are encased in
Word and sacrament. Whether John intended to or not, chap-*

59

*ter 6 turns out to be a penetrating biblical analysis and expla-
nation of the Mass where Jesus is present to believers in the
liturgy of the Word and in the liturgy of the sacrament. Perhaps
the following reflective commentary on the chapter can throw
some additional light on Jesus as the Bread of Life (and hopefully provide a deeper understanding and appreciation of the
Mass).*[1]

The Old Testament has often been called salvation history.
The God of Israel is one who *saves* and *liberates* his people
from their enemies. He calls them to share in his life through
loving faith and obedience to his will (revealed especially in
the Law). As they continue to believe and obey in love, he continues to save them with his providence and care. Their history began with Abraham, but it came into sharpest focus with
Moses and the Exodus. The Moses-Exodus-Passover event is
the centerpiece of the Old Testament. It shows conclusively
that the Lord of Israel is a saving God. Through his prophet
Moses he saved his people from bondage in Egypt and led them
to freedom and deeper covenant by giving them his Law at
Sinai-Horeb.

Little wonder, then, that Jesus, if he is to convince Israel
that he, and not Moses, is God's intended centerpiece in the
history of salvation, must fulfill, indeed transcend Moses and
all the saving events of Exodus-Passover. And so in chapter
6, near Passover, Jesus will show that he is the fulfillment of
this Old Testament mystery. The chapter is filled with motifs
that indicate Jesus is a new, better, more saving instrument
for God than Moses. In the first four verses Jesus parallels the
actions of Moses at Exodus: like Moses he "crosses the sea,"
with "large crowds following him." "They are attracted by his
signs." Jesus like Moses ascends "the mountain." In the verses
that follow, as Moses fed the Israelites with *manna* in the desert,

---

1. This appendix, with slight alterations, is taken from *JOHN: The Different Gospel:
A Reflective Commentary* by Michael J. Taylor, S.J. (New York: Alba House, 1983)
61–72 and is reprinted with permission.

Jesus provides barley bread to feed thousands (his fourth sign, vv. 5-13). As Moses spoke of a prophet to come (Deut 18:18), Jesus will be acknowledged by the crowd as that prophet actually come (v. 14). As Moses and his God saw the Israelites safely through the rough seas of Exodus, so Jesus walks on the waters (his fifth sign) and brings his disciples safely across the sea of Tiberias (vv. 16-21), hinting as he does, that he is very closely linked to Moses' God, *egō eimi* (v. 20). Even Jesus meets with the "murmuring" Moses experienced in the desert (vv. 41-42; 60-61).

The feast of Passover summoned up expectations of another liberating and saving prophet to come, a new Moses as it were for the New and Final Age. He was expected to free the Israelites from their present enemies and give them a more lasting manna to sustain them. Jesus in this chapter will speak with greater authority than Moses or any prophet and will announce that he not only can give the expected new manna, but that he himself *is* that manna, bread come from heaven, which if eaten gives eternal life. No doubt about it, as Jesus earlier in the Gospel absorbed into himself the purifying waters of the Old Testament (ch. 2), as he cleansed and replaced the Temple (ch. 2), as he made it possible for the born of Abraham and Adam to be born of the Spirit (chs. 3, 4), as he took over with the Father's approval the life-giving works of the sabbath (ch. 5), so here in chapter 6, Jesus begins to take over (since he has one more Passover to go) the Moses-Exodus-Passover event, replacing it with a new, better, eternal bread from heaven and giving Israel a new Moses whose Exodus-Passover is to lead to the literal life and land of the Father.

Multiplication of the Loaves: 6:5-13

Jesus' fourth sign, the multiplication of the loaves, appears in all the Gospels. This commonly narrated miracle must have had special significance for early Christians. Many scholars think they saw it as a prophetic anticipation of the Eucharist, which from the beginning was one of the distinctive liturgical acts of Christians (cf. Acts 2:42-46). Catacomb paintings bear out an early linking of the two. The miracle seems in fact to be narrated by all evangelists in quasi-liturgical style: Jesus "looks up," and "blesses the loaves," "breaks them," "distributes them," "gathers the fragments left over" (all Eucharistic rubrical actions). John retains these liturgical aspects as he tells the story. In addition he mentions the miracle takes place near Passover, seeming to infer that the Eucharist, which became the Christian Passover meal, is prophesied in this sign. But it would only be later (with post-Easter reflection) that Christians would pick up the Eucharistic symbolism of the miracle. The immediate viewers are impressed mainly with the *wonder* of it. They look at the surface meaning of the sign: Jesus providing abundant earthly bread for earthly hunger. They do not see in his words and actions that he comes from God and is sent to give bread that will satisfy a deeper interior hunger for God. Jesus' signs are always and mainly that—revelations of who he is and what he can do for the world; the visible symbol encases his spiritual identity and functions. But most of the crowd see only the earthly effect, and since their views of messiahs and prophets to come are very earthly, they see Jesus as a provider of material food only. And the Jews expected this "prophet" to be more than a good provider; they envisioned him as a political deliverer (Passover seemed to intensify hopes of political liberation from Rome) and so the upshot of Jesus' remarkable sign is that they want to make him their prophet-king in a nationalistic sense (vv. 14-15). Jesus, however, is not their desired prophet-king. He is a prophet in God's sense—one who reveals God and his will. He is a king who will liberate and rule the world spiritually through the giving of his flesh and blood.

Jesus Walks on the Waters: 6:16-21

The evening of the day Jesus multiplied the bread, he works

his fifth sign. Jesus normally explains the deeper meaning of his signs, and we might wonder why he walks on the waters before explaining the meaning of the bread-sign. But in John's thinking the explanation of Jesus as the "bread from heaven" (which will be revealed in vv. 35-58) can only be understood if one accepts him as the Word come from heaven. Jesus can give better bread than Moses because he is greater than Moses in a remarkable way. He is the *incarnation* of the son of Moses' God (who since the time of Exodus has also been known as *egō eimi*). *Egō eimi* was with Moses and the Israelites during the first Exodus, getting them safely through the seas from Egypt to Sinai. Jesus must show that in him believers can find and hear the mystery of *egō eimi* also. The Moses-Exodus-Passover motif continues: it is night—it is dark—the seas are rough (vv. 16-18). As *egō eimi* came to the Israelites of old, so Jesus, "sent" by *egō eimi*, comes to the new Israelites, the disciples, and gets them safely across the sea (cf. Exod 14; Pss 77:19; 78:13). Knowing the "divine origins and power" of Jesus, the disciples will be able to accept the divine claims that will be made in the Bread of Life Discourse.

Verses 22-24 make up a transitional passage to get the witnesses of the multiplication miracle and others to Capernaum where Jesus is to deliver his Bread of Life Discourse. Scholars see the verses as awkwardly put together and think John is telescoping two or more events into a sequential story. To understand the discourse, the reader should see it in the context of these two signs; thus John brings the audiences of the signs into the synagogue where the discourse is to be given. The signs and the discourse are theologically connected and so must be witnessed by the *same people.*

Verses 25-34, a rabbinical debate carried on between Jesus and the crowd, provide a lead-in to the Bread of Life Discourse. The crowd wonders how Jesus arrived at Capernaum without a boat (believers and all who look at his signs with open, seeing eyes know how Jesus is able to accomplish this). But Jesus informs them that they look only at the surface of what he does, and so see only that he has power to provide earthly food (v. 26). That food lasts only a short while, just as human life lasts only so long. Jesus transcends earthly food and human life. He can give eternal life and sustain it; his bread is of a different transcendental category, yet these people seek him only for perishable food to sustain their perishable lives.

Verse 27 reminds them the Father backs up Jesus' claim. The two signs of the chapter joined with the others of the Gospel indicate the Father works in tandem with Jesus. The trouble is, many are not doing the work (vv. 27, 28, 29) that would help them see Jesus has access to bread from above. They must open their eyes and hearts to his actions and words. The essential work they must do to penetrate Jesus' identity and power is this: they must look at and listen to him with total openness and with no preconditions. People should not tell Jesus what he can do and who he should be. They should let *him* do his thing and say his piece. They should listen to him as he tells them who he is. He (and the Gospel generally) told them he is one sent by God and that he is not the provider of earthly food only. He has told them he was sent by God to give new life. If they believed that, then the signs will show what he says is true. They encase in visible symbols the truth of his words.

But the crowd is nowhere near that openness or faith, and so again it seeks only earthly groceries from Jesus. Some quote Scripture as a "come-on" for a do-it-again multiplication miracle. They recall that their ancestors were given manna in the desert to eat: "He gave them bread from heaven to eat" (Exod 16:4, 15; Ps 78:23; Wis 16:26). The ancient manna, though earthly, is actually "bread from heaven" they argue. God through Moses gave it to them, and Jesus, if he is really Moses' prophet, should give it to them *again;* that is their rabbinical interpretation of the Old Testament text quoted in verse 31. Jesus (a good rabbi too) counters with his own interpretation of the text. The bread from heaven that God was talking about is none other than Jesus himself; that text was a prophecy of him. It explains who Jesus is and why he comes. The Gospel from the beginning has described Jesus as the Word of God. God's Word in the Old Testament was often described as food or bread (cf. Amos 8:11-13; Prov 9:4-6; Sir 15:3; 24:21). Jesus, then, is God's food, God's bread sent from heaven, and such a bread or word is always life-giving, more so than any earthly bread (cf. Deut 8:2-3; Wis 16:26). A flashback to earlier chapters and a "flash forward" to coming chapters will show that Jesus' signs in John are all life-giving in character. And in his discourses Jesus often indicates the life in his signs is symbolic of the life he brings from above. It is a visible encasement of that life. Hearing Jesus offer bread that gives imperishable life, they ask for it (v. 34). Jesus informs them in clear terms that he is the bread that gives imperishable life to the world. This bread is theirs to have if they would believe.

Bread of Life Discourse: 6:35-58 (59)

We recall the crowd in verse 31 gave Jesus his discourse text ("he gave them bread from heaven to eat"). Jesus has already explained the he in the text is his Father and not Moses. Since Jesus has been described often as the "one sent from God," the implication is that Jesus is the bread from heaven. But this must be stated clearly. Jesus begins his revealing statement with the dramatic *egō eimi,* indicating what he is about to say is not just good rabbinic interpretation—it is God's interpretation of the text. He clearly identifies himself as the heavenly bread of life (v. 35).

Since the coming verses of the discourse (51b-58, 59) are obviously Eucharistic in meaning, it has often been thought that the bread Jesus speaks about in verses 35-51a is also intended to be Eucharistic in meaning. Most scholars, however, now agree that these initial verses refer to Jesus mainly as bread in a Wisdom sense (again, cf., Prov 9:4-6; Sir 15:3; 24:21; Wis 16:26). Jesus is describing himself as the Old Testament described Wisdom. Indeed all of God's revelations in the Old Testament, including the Law, were spoken of as God's food or bread sent from heaven. Jesus, then, in these verses is describing himself as the bringer of God's Word, his message of love, his plan for the world. If one accepts him as sent by God and embraces his message, one will "know" the life that is in God. His words are not just information about God. They contain or encase in a perceivable way the mystery of God and the life within God. When one listens openly and accepts his words sincerely, one experiences his presence, life, and love. Jesus in these early verses seeks the key response all people must give to God's Word (God's self-revealing Wisdom)—faith, openness, and readiness to believe what God says. If Jesus receives this he can satisfy people's hunger and thirst for a sharing in God's life (v. 35). Those who listen to and accept his words will never be forsaken (v. 37); they will have eternal life (v. 40); they will be raised up on the last day (vv. 39, 40).

The Father is key to Jesus' self-identification (vv. 35-40), for Jesus is his Word. Jesus does not speak only his own thoughts and plans for the world; his are identical to the Father's. Some of those present in the original audience at the synagogue *and* some in and near John's Church (c. A.D. 90-95) doubt that Jesus' words are also the Father's. John must make it clear that Jesus *and* the Father both identify Jesus as the bread from heaven. No one can say they have the Father's bread and do not need Jesus. Jesus *is* the bread the Father gives to the world (v. 33). His words encase God's "nourishing" life.

But this is so hard for "surface observers" of Jesus to see. How can he be the Father's bread sent from heaven, when earthly evidence identifies his origins as not from heaven but from Nazareth, from Joseph (vv. 41-42)? If they had taken his words as truly spoken, if they had looked more deeply at his signs and opened their hearts fully to his words, they would discover Jesus' "higher origins." But again these verses indicate they cannot take Jesus at his word; what he says and does originates only from a human source, and so as the Israelites reacted with incredulity to Moses (Exod 16:2, 7-8), the crowd "murmurs" against Jesus' self-identification as the bread the Father sends from heaven (vv. 41-42).

Being himself so convinced of Jesus' divine origins, John must have wondered why so many people refused then and during his own time to see what he so clearly sees. John, as Jewish dualist, knows that free human beings have two options and this to some degree answers the riddle of rejection. But the option for Jesus is so attractive, so compelling that John still is hard put to know why so many do not choose Jesus. Verses 44-50 give him part of the mysterious answer he seeks. He finds it in Isa 54:13. These people are not listening as deeply as they should to the Father of Jesus. He is discoverable in the Scriptures; they prepare Israel for Jesus (v. 45). But to accept Jesus, one not only needs openness, one also needs some help, some "grace" from the Father to discover that Jesus is his bread from heaven. The Father is not standing silently by hoping the world will accept his son; he is drawing the world to him through the Scriptures and through his attracting grace. It can only be that many do not look honestly and deeply into the Scriptures and that many reject his attracting grace. To John, the strong dualist, it must be that many are blinding themselves to the Father's "evidence" for Jesus (ch. 9 of the Gospel explicitly shows this to be the case).

Many rejected Jesus (despite his miracles) because, in comparison to Moses, he did not quite measure up to the glories and glamor of Moses and Exodus. Since God in their view seems more obviously with Moses, they opt to stay with him (some of John's people actually seem to be leaving Christ and returning to "Moses," i.e., going back to the synagogue). Jesus (and John) answer those taking the "Moses option" by saying "that one (viz., Moses) has not *seen* the Father." It is dangerous to choose Moses over Jesus, for Jesus "is from God and has *seen* the Father" (v. 46). In retrospect Christians know that Moses' manna was only earthly bread, and his revelations were not end-of-the-line revelations, but anticipations of Jesus. To return to him would be to settle for a half-told, half-fulfilled story and for earthly bread only.

Johannine realized eschatology, so strong in verses 35–40,

emerges again in strong terms as Jesus concludes the "Wisdom" portion of his discourse. If one at all doubts that faith in Jesus has value for the present (over and above the Old Testament and the earthly manna it offers), Jesus assures those who believe in him and his message (the bread he brings) that they are in possession of eternal life now (v. 47). Unlike those who hope for another earthly manna that cannot keep them alive for long, believers *now* possessing the bread-life of Jesus' Word are never to die (vv. 49-50).

The sapiential character of verses 35-51a is evident to many commentators from the response Jesus seeks. "Eating" does not specifically enter the discourse until verse 50, and from then on until verse 58 verbs that denote eating predominate. Here in verses 35-51a Jesus seeks the response of faith to his words. The verbs are all synonyms for faith: e.g., Jesus wants people to come to him (used five times), to believe in him (used four times), to look upon, to be drawn to, to hear, to learn, to be taught by the Father. It seems, then, in the earliest form of chapter 6 that the discourse was primarily intended to identify Jesus as the life-giving sapiential bread.

With verses 51b-58 (59) Jesus speaks of himself in another way than as Word. The meaning of bread in these verses seems obviously to be Eucharistic. These verses would be artificial to a discourse given this early in Jesus' ministry. Their meaning could only be understood in the context of the Last Supper. So what John has apparently done in these verses is artificially to move the "data" of the Last Supper to chapter 6 (John, by the way, will not include the institution of the Eucharist in his Last Supper account, chs. 13-17). Jesus' discourse here is meant especially for the Church of John and those with whom his Church is engaged in debate about the meaning and value of Jesus. Jesus is now (c. A.D. 90–95) understood to be the "bread from heaven" in two ways: he is God's Wisdom bread still teaching believers God's life-giving message through the Spirit, and he is with them in the Eucharistic bread received in the supper each first day of the week. If Jesus is understood to be these two breads, then he should speak of himself as such in the same discourse (this seems to be John's rationale for moving the material here). Thus, in a later version of the sapiential bread discourse, John (and/or his editors) inserted these verses (51b-58, 59) to show Jesus is also with believers in the Eucharistic bread (v. 56).

John's people need and must accept Jesus as both breads. The opponents of Jesus (c. A.D. 90-95) deny he was ever Wisdom from heaven and that he is in the Eucharistic bread where supposedly (God forbid) his "body and blood are eaten." It must be established for believers and non-believers alike that Jesus himself taught this, so that members of John's Church can firmly believe this truth and defend it vigorously before those who deny it. Wisdom never spoke of herself as "flesh to be eaten" (bread, yes; flesh, no); it is Jesus at the Last Supper who said this. Flesh or blood will be used ten times in this section; eating, drinking, feeding on will be used ten times also. When can Jesus have said this except at the Last Supper? To eat the bread of Wisdom means to accept and believe her *words*. To eat and drink the flesh and blood of Jesus can only mean to accept his personal love present in the symbols which Jews can legitimately eat and drink, namely, the Eucharistic symbols of bread and wine.

Jesus speaks here on a deep spiritual level. His hearers understand him on a very surface earthly level. In surface meaning, to eat flesh and blood is incomprehensible to Jews and in fact unlawful (cf. Lev 17:11-12), but on the spiritual level of meaning Jesus can very definitely invite believers to "eat" of the deeper meaning of "his flesh and blood" for the words idiomatically mean his "offered life and love." Jesus is not making cannibals of believers (v. 53). He is making them symbol-partakers of his loving transcendental presence by inviting them to share in the meaningful meal-symbols of bread and wine. These were the symbols he chose at the Last Supper to be the encasement of his given life and love. Jesus has not only given believers his words to live by; he has given them himself, his life, his body crushed, his blood poured out—in other words the loving act of his death—to live by and has made it available to them in the Eucharistic symbol of bread (v. 56). They must *hear* and *listen* to Jesus (the sapiential bread), but just as importantly, they must know that they have Jesus with them in the Eucharistic bread. Lovers must speak to one another surely, but lovers must have each other, must "touch" one another. This is necessary *bread* too (v. 55). People are body-spirit beings and communicate love to each other mainly through the symbols of *word* and *touch* and so Jesus has given them himself in both symbols, both forms—the word *and* the touch.

It is a tragedy of Christian history that Christians thought they could get along with one while ignoring the other. Perhaps John teaches modern believers as much as he taught his own people, Christians to be fully nourished need both the bread of the Word and the bread of the sacrament. They cannot survive on less. Jesus must speak to them and they to him, but each must also touch the other. How else are they really to know and feel how close Jesus wants to be to them; how else know what this lofty term "eternal life" is all about? And since Word was heard and the Eucharist eaten weekly in a community setting, the reader knows that John understands Word and sacrament to be Jesus' principal bread-gifts to his Church.

Moreover, when Jesus says the Eucharistic bread contains his "blood," readers know that Jesus as a Jew understands it to mean the bread encases the mystery of his "life" (life is in the blood). To be forgiven of sin, Jews had to symbolically give their life in penitence to God; this they did by giving their "blood" symbolically in the blood of an offered animal. Now sinners know that the "blood" Jesus gives in the Eucharist contains his life and it is in his giving of self that they can know forgiveness of sins. Thus the Eucharist is not only experiencing the "touch" of Christ; it is feeling the "forgiving touch" of Christ.

Jesus repeats what he said of himself as Wisdom (v. 50):

that those who eat of his Eucharistic bread will never know death (v. 58). Jesus is exceptionally categorical about the "eating of his body" (said eight times). This obviously reflects a dispute his Church is having (with itself and others) over the presence of Jesus in the bread-symbol—difficult for non-Jesus people to believe; difficult for Jesus people to believe; still fully believable because the Jesus who says it is indeed from heaven. Surely if human beings can encase their love in human symbols, all the more can God's Word do so. In fact, Jesus is much better at it than they will ever be, since they often claim to be in the symbols of their love—the kiss, the squeeze, the hug, etc., when often they are not. Jesus, the truly authentic one from heaven, can never be absent from the symbols he chooses to encase his love in. If he, God's Word incarnate, says his love, his Body given, his Blood shed, is in the bread, then most certainly believers know that it is there.

With verse 60 the chapter takes up again where an earlier form of the discourse left off in verse 51a, where Jesus first mainly spoke of himself as the sapiential bread from heaven. This of course scandalizes those who regard Jesus on the level of the human only and who see no "divine connection" in him at all (a connection revealed in the two signs of the chapter). He (some have said) is *only* the son of Joseph, only human, and as such must be (c. A.D. 90-95) dead. But Jesus must remind them his history did not cease with his death. The Jesus of this Gospel, besides being God's Word who descended, is also the incarnate Word who ascended and whose Spirit has been sent to believers (vv. 62-64). Jesus is not just the human son of Joseph; as such he could not feed them with eternal life: "the flesh is useless" (v. 63). He is the ascended one and therefore can make good and has made good on his boast to give believers the life of one ascended to God.

Sadly John recounts that some disciples (of superficial faith) broke away from Christ, apparently having chosen to return to "Moses" and the synagogue. This undoubtedly is happening to John's Church (it seems mainly because of John's "high"

Christology, Christ is professed to be true bread from heaven. Also the "high" sacramentology of his Church places Jesus *really* in the bread and wine of the Eucharist). Knowing the "facts" of his Gospel, John is in a quandary why people cannot accept this. His refuge again is in the mystery of belief. Even though the option of belief is open to all, it is not easy to believe. The Judas-enigma must have repeated itself many times in John's Church (vv. 64, 70-71). All need the help of the Father (v. 65). To follow Christ is *grace* as well as *option*. It seems to be John's conclusion that some willfully reject that help and are not listening to Jesus' key witness, the Father (cf. ch. 5). Having lost some followers, Jesus now turns to Peter to learn of his reaction to the identification of himself as the bread from heaven. Does he believe this to be true? Speaking for John's Church (and doubtless reflecting a more mature, post-resurrection faith of that Church), Peter (who witnessed both of the chapter's signs and saw in them "epiphanies" of a true bread from heaven) acknowledges his belief in and acceptance of the revelation (vv. 68-69): "Lord, to whom can we turn? You are the one with words of eternal life."